Statistically Speaking

A Poetry Collection

Dr. Caroline Lauture-Azeb

BookLeaf Publishing

India | USA | UK

To my fellow Black and Brown sisters;

This is an ode to you.

I see you. I honor you. I love you.

Keep fighting, I need you.

Acknowledgement

I am appreciative for the friendships, relationships, and lessons I have gained—and even those I have lost— throughout my journey. I am grateful for my husband, family, and loved ones for all of their support, honor, and grace.

Most of all, I am eternally grateful to the young girl I was who stood firm in her beliefs, to the young adult I became who lost her way but found the strength to return, and to the woman I am today—still growing, still healing, and still becoming her best self.

Preface

I chose to write this novel to share my experiences with the hope of freeing myself from the burden of holding everything in, and of inspiring those who have faced or are going through similar experiences. With every word I typed in this novel, I felt the freedom that came with it.

I didn't allow the idea of perfection to win. I wrote with intentionality and authenticity. I ended each line with a period, whether it was a run on or not, because this symbolized the course my life took. Every interaction, every conversation, every emotion, every moment—ended. Sometimes, they ended abruptly.

Writing this novel allowed me to finally release the pain and regret that has accompanied me my entire life, and to reminisce and sit in a lot of the joy, power and independence that also came with it. Here is to owning my pain, because I no longer want to live there.

Soulmates

It was always just the five of us.
We weren't considered cool or popular, but
everyone knew us.
We knew us.
We went from scheduled nap times to
researching dinosaurs and sharks.
We went from playing house to racing one
another during recess.
We went from talking about hair to talking
about our crushes.

We were inseparable.
We were each other's soulmates. Or so, that's
what we thought.
We became pre-teens, and before we knew it,
puberty hit.

We were still close, though some bonds
tightened more than others.
We always had each other's backs, that never
changed.
We always fought ferociously for one another,
never letting them mess with us.

By the time 8th grade came around, we knew
this was it.
Soon would come the day that we would call
it quits.
Strange how things go, and people grow
apart.
20 years later and I can still feel my broken
heart.

My First Love

We were about eight years old and in love.
I'd say me, far more than you.
The only thing you were focused on at that
age was recess games with your friends and
acting a fool.

A glance here.
A soft smile there.
Man, was I crushing hard.
I knew then that I wanted you to be my first
kiss.
So, we planned it.

All day my palms were sweating, and I swore
you could hear my heart beating.
In the basement halls of a Catholic school.
Where they kept all of the long brown tables.
A narrow space connecting the boy's and
girl's bathroom.
The time was set.

Our closest friends kept look out.
We did it.

It was official-official.
You were mine, and I was yours.
That was, until the end of the school year.
You never came back, you moved away.
I lost my first love, the one I prayed would stay.

My First Time

We were close, closer than most.
From braiding each other's hair to sharing
food.
We finished each other's sentences; we were
so in tune.

I don't remember whose idea it was.
It just came up in conversation.
"You want to try something different?"
I couldn't resist the temptation.

So, we raised our hands to use the bathroom.
We were sure to stagger the times.
We laid on the cold concrete in the back of
one of the stalls.

It didn't matter that we were best friends.
It didn't matter that we were both girls.
We wanted to do everything together.
We wanted to touch and taste the world.

The Bully

You were never a nice person.
Rotten from the inside out.
Your thick, coarse hair in bubbles, doodoo
braids
and multicolored barrettes to blend in like
the rest of us.
You were short.
Your nose hairs made their appearance known
with little to no effort from the wide nose
that housed them.
Your personality was big, it covered up your
insecurities,
but your words loomed even larger.

I was never mean to you, always cordial.
I never considered you a friend and maybe
that was the root of the problem.

You made sure you mocked everything about
me, from head to toe.
You rolled your eyes whenever I spoke.
You snickered when I walked by.

You turned the rest of the girls against me,
and they never cared to ask why.

So, I stuck to my core group of friends, the
Fab Five.
We always had each other's back; we would
always be each other's ride or die.
They made that year more bearable; Without
them, I never would've survived it.

You made my 4th grade year miserable, and I
will never forgive you.
It was my first taste of bullying, but it
wouldn't be the last.
Even though you left at the end of the school
year, you set the tone for the torment that
followed the next four.

I hate you forever. Ain't shit in the past.

Rounding Out

The sharp pain radiated from the top of my
breastbone to the fatty tissue at the bottom.
It was followed by a throbbing but also dull
sensation.
My areolas were enlarged, hot to the touch.

I checked my calendar.
Could it be my period?
No.
Did I bump my chest last night?
No.

I went into the bathroom and there they
were.
Two limes, their pointy edges staring back at
me.
I smiled so hard; I had to squeeze my cheeks
to stop the tingling.

Breasts.

At 13, I finally had breasts.

They're not as big as I expected, but hell it
was a start.
I finally had breasts to go with my round ass.
I finally caught up to the other girls in my 8th
grade class.

I put on my psychedelic low-cut shirt with
some jeans and flats,
fully prepared to strut into the classroom to
show off.
Everyone was shocked.
I could feel the jealousy perched on my chest.
So, I kept it pushing, my foot on their necks.

The Predator

As we sang Vitamin C's graduation song, our
eyes connected.
I felt a rush of heat in places I never
anticipated.
This is it. This is our moment.

But my Momma knew better.
She knew nothing good was coming.
I didn't listen; I chose to follow my heart.
By the end of the night, you had my number,
and I had yours.

A few years difference between you and me.
I'd been crushing on since the 5th grade when
you made me a deal:
"Let's keep this a secret, no one can know.
I'll be back for you, be sure you're ready to
go."

From that moment on, my life changed.
There were many happy moments but there
were some full of shame.

You used me as a pawn in your little game of
chess.
Damn you— and the damage you left.
You made a real fucking mess.

Lies to keep me around, feeding into my
romance fantasies
while you kept another girl.
Mind games that bred codependency,
tricking me into believing every wound was
proof of love—something real.

Your lies forced me to lie to those I loved.
It caused a hemorrhage no drugs would have
healed.
Those relationships died right on the table.
I'd been pouring into us since the age of 13,
while you groomed me to be the woman you
wanted—
silent, hidden, unseen.

Losing it, Twice

Sophomore year, I was 16 years old.
I thought I was grown, yet mostly did what I
was told.
A high performing student, advanced courses,
JV tennis,
clubs, and undetermination.

This day, I skipped tennis practice and headed
home early.
Mom was working late, and little sis was with
other family.

In broad daylight I snuck you in.
Keyshia Cole's Love.
Pain, tears, blood,
hugging that led to our first dance,
in my shared room where my Usher, TLC,
and G-Unit posters stared.

Fast forward to senior year.
On Senior Skip Day, we drove to your place.
I took my first puff and lungs filled with
smoke.

Another first that I gave you, while you left
my hand empty.
Fuck.
How could you?

The Last Time

At my locker, right before lunch, I ended our
friendship.
I made things abundantly clear.
You lied.
You shared my secrets with those who hated
me.
You couldn't keep up
so, you thought shame would tame me.
One thing you forgot—
God don't like ugly.

You'd pay for your indiscretions loud and
unforgiving.
When people found out we no longer
associated,
they cheered—relieved the truth, no longer
hidden in darkness has seen the light. See, I
was always loyal to you, but you had other
plans.

They shared things you said about me,
things I never knew, they knew how deep my
loyalty ran,
they knew I wouldn't believe you unless they
had proof.
Grateful I saw it with my own two eyes,
our friendship over, your loyalty poisoned.

You couldn't let me go
so, you all followed me to the store.
Harassed me into answering why, the cashier
was tempted to call the police.
Then at graduation I waited until the diploma
was in my hand.
The good girl, high-achieving student, was
ready to throw hands.

Leaving Home

It was the permission to go that you took
away.
My anger grew.
It was the way you effortlessly snapped
"Because I said so."
My anger grew.

I decided in that moment that I had a choice
to make.
Me or you.
My anger grew.

That was it. I had enough.
I put my foot down.
"I am going," I declared.
It was my first official date.
He was already waiting outside.

You blocked the door so I wouldn't pass.
Words were exchanged.
English from me.
Haitian Creole from you.

"Kochon".
"Salopri".

It escalated.
You called everyone.
You said I put my hands on you.
I didn't. I raised my voice.

I said you slammed my head against the door.
I threatened to call the police.
You denied it.

"CALL THEM!" you yelled.
"Let them take you away."
My anger grew.

Leaving Home
Continued

I went into my shared bedroom.
I called him to let him know what was going
on.
You came in, continuing your rant.
You became so irate that you lost it.

The pure rage in your eyes was unlike
anything I had ever seen from you.
But guess what? So were mine.
You jumped on me.
Held my hands down, screaming and pushing
me into the bed.
You were trying to get your way by any means
necessary.
My anger exploded.

I pushed you off of me while my sisters
watched and cried.
With the help of your boyfriend, he pulled
you to the side.

He didn't agree with what you did but you
refused to hear it.
You said, "I am an adult and you're the
child–you need to listen."
My anger exploded.

I packed my bags, said goodbye to my sisters.
My heart was breaking, my soul blistered.
When I got to his car you three begged me to
come back.
You looked out the window silently, and I
knew then there was no turning back.

The First Loss

You were in the shower.
I made a joke while I peed on the stick.
We were surprised.
Then shit hit the fan.

I stared at the promise ring that was planned
to be replaced.
I touched my belly in amazement, imagining
your warm embrace.

Three months of insurance calls, fighting,
crying, late nights and hiding.
I was a full-time student still taking classes,
nauseous, hungry–
You'd leave me starving.

You had control over things like money.
So, you thought you'd starve her or him out.
You constantly texted me, tracked me, made
me feel unworthy.

My friend warned me this was abuse, get away
now before it's too late.
I assured her that it's just because he loves
me.

A Loss in Waiting

Three months in, still torn by indecision.
That day you threw me on the bed and
screamed "SHUT UP!" while I was arguing
with you.
You threw your Blackberry against the wall; it
broke in half.
You punched the wall behind the door.
You were beyond mad.

I cried all day, scared, paralyzed by fear..
I decided that day that I wanted no parts of
you.
The decision has been made as well as the
appointment.
You handed me a letter you wrote to our
unborn child
I froze, undecided.

We get to the clinic, you pay cash.
Can't leave a paper trail while you take out
your trash.
I open the pamphlet, the one they say not to
read.

As I read every word, my heart takes a
beating.
His fingers, Her toes, they're already forming.

A Loss in Waiting
Continued

Seconds before calling my name, you turn to
me and say,
"You don't have to do this anymore. Let's just
leave instead"

The damage has been done.
My feelings remain unchanged.
I got up and walked to the back, realizing I
was breaking the chains.

The nurse walked out and told me what was
next.
I looked at the monitor, despite knowing I
shouldn't have.
I wept so fiercely, I felt my chest pushing
through the hospital gown.
I mourned.
I cried.
I mourned.
I cried.
I mourned.

I cried.
I mourned.
The loss of your life.
The loss of mine.

The Loss Finale

Medication.
Stabbing pain.
Medication.
Stabbing pain.
Medication.
Stabbing pain.
Cold, metallic bed beneath my spine.
The vacuum roared, deafening, unbearable.
The tube stretched long, unfitting.
"Don't look," they said.
"Don't look," I thought.
I looked.
Your eyes.
I screamed.
I cried; I mourned.

I screamed.
I cried; I mourned.
I screamed.
I cried; I mourned.
I screamed.
I cried; I mourned.

Two nurses pinned me down.
Injected me with something.

Recovery was ruthless and unforgiving.
Hours passed beyond the predicted time,
Still bleeding heavily.
"Emergency room is a possibility," they
warned.
No, no, no, no, no.
I just needed more time.

I crawled into the car.
I crawled into the bed.
I closed my eyes and wished it was me in that
vacuum instead.

The I'm Sorry He Bought

Cooking us dinner in your parents' kitchen.
I turned around when I heard the screen
door.

A furry head and a sharp yelp ran right to me.
I scooped you up and gave you kisses.
It felt like you had always known me.

"Surprise!" you said.
I knew what this was.
I swallowed hard and it pushed it away.
The swell of regret I carried that day.

Welcome home, Ace.

He Did It

It was Thanksgiving morning.
I stayed over to help cook.
We were sleeping head to feet, like cousins
usually do.
He was out cold, snoring loudly—he didn't
hear you.

You slithered your way into the bed, on my
side, close to the wall.
You were on your cell, talking to someone.
I was groggy, trying to figure out what was
happening.
And then I felt it. I understood then.

As your hand slid into my pants, past my
underwear,
I held my breath.
I wanted to scream, kick, bite, punch.
I couldn't move.
You continued your conversation on the
phone, while you violated me.

Suddenly, hearing your voice snapped me
back to reality.
It gave me enough strength to silently push
your hand off.

I pushed it off.
You put it back.
You kept talking on the phone.

I pushed it off.
You put it back.
You kept talking on the phone.

I pushed it off.
You put it back.
You kept talking on the phone.

You finally got up.
Left the room, like nothing happened.

I tried to wake my cousin up.
It took a few tries.
I told him what happened.
He didn't seem too surprised.

I locked myself in the bathroom.
Got ready for the day.
You tried to jiggle the door open.
I jumped and let you know I was in it.

I wanted to keep this to myself but something
in me couldn't.
I told one of my aunts when I arrived at her
house.
We cried before calling my mom.
They stood beside me and held me up,
reminding me I had done nothing wrong.

What do you want to do?
I want to tell my aunt, his wife–he's scum.
The conversation didn't go as planned.
She chose his side in the end.

I decided to speak up for myself and girls like
me.
I brought it to the courts. They took his side
as well.
See, I had to be raped to prove he violated
me.
That ruling dragged me straight into hell.

For years, well into my 30's I showered three
times a day.
I needed to get him off of me, I needed him
scrubbed away.
I would flinch when men would touch me.
Stored the assault in the back of my mind.
I wanted to erase what happened.
I wanted it back.
I wanted my life.

Searching for Home

I broke things off with no plan on where to
go or what to do.
I needed to get out.
I needed to get away from you.
I moved in with my friend for about a week,
until I could find my own place.

The manipulation.
The lies.
The grooming has come to an end.

I will stand on my own.
I will no longer pretend.

Eight years later, enough was enough.
I chose me.
I chose true love.

Finding My Way

I never stayed long.
6 months.
A year.
Every scum lord I encountered never made it
easy.

Everything was a first for me.
Learning as I go.
Deciding which bills to pay first, to eat or lay
low.

I was barely making ends meet.
I had school, a full-time job and a part time
job.
Still, it wasn't enough.

Did I make the right decision to leave him?
Yes. Yes, it was.
There were cold nights where I had to turn on
the stove.
Cuddling Ace to keep our bodies warm.
The heat had to stay low.
I ate noodles or pizza for dinner.

The struggle, never shown.

I played it off well.
I didn't have a choice.
I hustled every day, doing what I could to see
my money grow.
I lived with roaches.
I lived with mice.
I lived with criminals.
From bullet holes in the walls.
To dog ears getting cut right in the kitchen.

I never stayed long.
6 months.
A year.
Every scum lord I encountered never made it
easy.

I was on a payment plan for everything and
anything.
I didn't give a shit.
I needed to keep a roof over my head, even if I
was drowning.
I convinced myself I needed to make it.

From the Train to My Front Porch

The doors chimed closed.
I am sitting with my 13-hour day heavy on my
face.
I felt strange and looked up.
There he was, staring, unblinking.
Goosebumps crawled up my arms,
And chills down my back.

After getting off the train, I got onto the bus.
I sat in the back so I could keep my eye on
him.
Something wasn't right.

I got off my stop.
I remembered what my mom told me a long
time ago.
I fumbled with my bag, pretending to search
for something, anything.
Giving him enough time to walk to his
destination.

To calm my anxiety that I was being
followed.
He did the same.

I crossed the street, called my boyfriend.
As I whispered what was happening.
He was mimicking my moves.
I walked faster; he walked faster.
I slowed down; he slowed down.
He's coming.
He crossed the street.
He's coming.
He stopped in front of my apartment.
He's coming.
We're staring at each other from across the
street.
He's coming.
RUN.

I take a left to run in the opposite direction.
I need to get back to the main road.
I turn.
He's behind me.
I run.
I turn.

He's gone.

He's gone.
He's gone.
He's gone.
He's gone.

Until next week.

Slowly Rebuilding a Bridge

The day I moved out of my apartment, you
were there.
We packed, laughed, and talked.

I told you everything.
The verbal abuse.
The emotional abuse.
The mental abuse.
The physical assault.
The pregnancy.
The abortion.
The poverty.

We cried.
We hugged.
We apologized.

We cried again.
We hugged again.
We apologized again.

We let go of the past.
Chose to move on and do better, be better for
one another.
For our future.
Although we bumped heads on how you
loved me.
You never stopped.
Thank you for loving me–unconditionally..

Mommy, I Love You.
In this life, and the next.

Holding My Head
Above Water

There were days I couldn't get out of bed.
I would call out of work.
I didn't move.
I didn't eat.
I barely talked.

Everything felt so heavy.
Heavy were my eyelids.
Heavy was my head.
Heavy were my arms.
Heavy were my legs.

It doesn't always look like this.
So obvious and in your face.
Sometimes I was happy and not a hair was
out of place.
I laughed at all the jokes and made plans to
see you later.
But I was swallowing water so fast, my lungs
ran out of air.

I was sinking fast.
I didn't know how to swim.
Would anyone send me a life vest?
And then you did.

So grateful for my village.
Who pulled me up whenever I was down.
Although some of you moved away or out of
my life, I knew you were around.
Thank you for being there wherever and
whenever I needed it.
Temporary or forever, that type of love
remains undefeated.

Sinking into the deep is not a one and done.
It's something to consistently work on.
It's a choice you make everyday.
Until you feel at home.
Until you feel safe.

Printed by Libri Plureos GmbH in Hamburg, Germany